SKI EASY...
The New Technique

SKI EASY...
The New Technique
Alpine and Cross-country

Ernie McCulloch

Foreword by Raymond Lanctôt

McGraw-Hill Ryerson Limited

Toronto   Montreal   New York   London   Sydney
Mexico   Johannesburg   Panama   Düsseldorf   Singapore
São Paulo   Kuala Lumpur   New Delhi

SKI EASY . . . THE NEW TECHNIQUE

ISBN 0-07-092777-4

Library of Congress Catalog Card No. 73-1193

2 3 4 5 6 7 8 9 10   BP-73   2 1 0 9 8 7 6 5 4 3

Printed and Bound in Canada

NO TOC

Contents

Foreword

"If you can fill the unforgiving minute
    With sixty seconds' worth of distance run,
Yours is the Earth and everything that's in it,
    And — which is more — you'll be a Man, my son!"

Kipling

More than a quarter-century of ski activities on the Canadian and international levels have given me many an occasion to pause to evaluate Kipling's "Ifs" in the world of skiing:

"If you can keep your head . . .

"If you can dream —

"If you can think —

"If you can meet with Triumph and Disaster . . .

"If you can make one heap of all your winnings
    And risk it on one turn of pitch-and-toss . . .

"And so hold on when there is nothing in you
    Except the Will which says to them: 'Hold on!' "

Exposure to the exigencies and rigors of skiing, to the cold and ice, to conquering the mountains, to the continuous tests of courage, to the anxieties and frustrations before realizing dreams and tasting glories, all go into the production of the ski champion.

It would be a thrill one day to evaluate the contributions to this sport by such colleagues as Emile Allais, James Coutet, Tony Sailer, Adrien Duvillard, and the grand master of modern French skiing, Jean Vuarnet, or, their Canadian counterparts, the gold medalists, Lucille Wheeler, Anne Heggtveit, Nancy Greene, the Austrian-born Herman Gadner, John Fripp, the Clifford brothers, Harvey and John, Peter Duncan and others. And conversely, perhaps of more importance, the role that skiing has played in moulding the character of these outstanding personalities.

For the moment, let's look at one of skiing's most scintillating personalities — Ernie McCulloch. Our paths first crossed some twenty-five years ago. How young he was! How young I was! The intervening years of association and friendship have given me ample opportunity to study and evaluate the skiing phenomenon that McCulloch has become. It has been a fortunate friendship; for viewing Ernie's varied contributions to the history of skiing, and skiing's moulding of an Ernie McCulloch have been rewarding experiences.

The result: a man who became a perceptive analyst of skiing technique, an impatient stylistic innovator, and yet a charming and enthusiastic instructor; a motivator of the youthful competitor; a teacher of teachers where his boundless zeal was frustrated often by the learner's ineptitude, often by a recalcitrant, out to bite the feeding hand. A man who coached champions, who has single-handedly expounded doctrines to international instructors' conferences, yet is never too busy to give of his immeasurable energy to improve the hopes of a mediocre racer or the prospects of an apprentice instructor.

No such helping hand was, nor could be, extended to the young bilingual product of an English family in a French-Canadian town when at sixteen he set out with only an ideal to guide him; an ideal to conquer the Alpine ski world, although no tradition or heritage of Alpine skiing existed in his family or home town. When the opportunity was ripe for this young competitor to test the world's best, was it not his own officious people who declared him ineligible by standards which were not respected by other skiing nations? Was it not his own ski school director at Sun Valley who assigned the nationally ranked competitor to teach beginner snowplow classes? And did not an ankle injury rob him of his chances for world glory when finally representing his country in Europe?

Through it all, the McCulloch resilience was formed, the ability to land on his feet, a renewal of the man to meet the circumstances. By work and desire, he forged his own road to success; establishing an F.I.S. international reputation as a competitor, officially presenting the Canadian Ski Instructors' technique to the World Congress of Instructors, developing a style of skiing, if at times showy, nevertheless electrifying and capable of paling by comparison the efforts of leading technique exponents of the day, a day in which "The King" meant McCulloch of Mont Tremblant, whose exploits superseded the existing folklore of that ancient mountain.

Now the McCulloch legend becomes more deeply engraved in the history of skiing, in a new book which demonstrates the author's ability not only to remain abreast of developments in technique, but to anticipate the rebirth of his first love — cross country skiing.

Our hats are again toffed to one of skiing's greats,

Bonjour Ernie,
Ton ami Raymond
Raymond Lanctôt

Introduction

It has been several years since my last book was published. Since that time there have been even further advances in equipment, ski techniques and methods of teaching. Photography has played a great part in the analysis of modern competitive and advanced skiing. With the use of high speed movie and still cameras it has been possible to analyze the movements of top skiers and competitors down to the most minute detail. This knowledge has been passed on to professional skiers, to ski schools, and thence to the general public, making it possible for anyone of intermediate ability to learn all of these advanced movements. While they may not be able to perform them as well as the champions, they will certainly improve their skiing and add to the enjoyment of the sport a great deal.

The level of skiing ability of the general public has vastly improved due to the growing number of ski clubs, clinics for children and teen-agers, more and more good ski schools, and the general popularity growth of skiing. There are travelling ski clinics for professionals to give instructors in more remote areas a chance to improve their knowledge of the newest techniques.

In this book I have tried to show as clearly and simply as possible the technique used in our school at Blue Mountain to teach not only beginners but intermediates and good skiers. I have gone into a great deal of detail in the advanced stages because I feel that most skiers of fair ability can learn these movements if they have the desire to do so and are willing to take advantage of the new teaching method. Many people who learned to ski a number of years ago and who can ski reasonably well down fairly difficult terrain seem to feel that there is no necessity for them to learn any more. Or some feel that they have been taught by old-fashioned methods and so cannot be taught the new technique. This is unfortunate because anything which is in this book can be learned by any skier of average ability, and if these advanced movements are mastered a whole new world will open up for the skier who has never felt the thrill of an avalement turn, an airborne turn, or skiing an extremely steep slope with edge set and rebound—or just the general mastering of all types of terrain in all kinds of snow conditions. Many people who ski reasonably well shy away from a steep, bumpy hill and yet such a hill can be skied quite easily once the person learns to do an edge set and a short radius turn. If the skier attempts to ski down such terrain by side slipping and trying to avoid the bumps he will not enjoy it very much and will even be afraid of such a hill another time.

In addition to the section on alpine skiing, I have included a rather lengthy discussion of the essentials of cross country skiing. As most skiers are aware, cross country is quite different from downhill skiing and requires different guidelines, instruction, and equipment. Since more and more winter sports enthusiasts are becoming interested in cross country skiing as conditioning for downhill or as an independent activity, the second part of this book is included to provide the skier with the essentials of good performance in both fields.

In all of the advanced sections of the book I have endeavoured to use more pictures than words because I have always felt that a great deal of technical terminology only confuses the average reader and discourages him from going on. In this connection I would like to give special thanks to photographer Toby Rankin who not only takes great photographs but understands skiing and is a pleasure to work with. I would also like to thank my wife, Janet, for her assistance with the text, and Northsport Ltd. for the use of their very fine ski equipment. I hope that this book will be of help to you and that it will encourage you to continue into the more advanced stages of skiing.

Part One
Alpine Skiing

Equipment

SKIS

Construction

Most good skis today are made of fibreglass or metal or a combination (fibreglass and metal, metal and wood, fibreglass and wood). Any one of these made by a well-known manufacturer should give good performance for any type of skier. Most high performance racing skis are made of fibreglass or fibreglass and wood because they respond somewhat faster than the other types of skis. Whatever type you decide upon, make certain that you choose the proper length for your height and weight and that the skis are of the right stiffness for you and have the right amount of camber.

The construction of skis has improved a great deal resulting in better performance as well as easier and quicker handling. Modern skis hold much better on a hard surface than those made a few years ago. The dampening qualities have improved cutting down on vibration and flutter and give you a much steadier ski.

Length

Because of improvements the tendency among better skiers is to ski on shorter skis than before. There was a time when you needed length for stability but because of the steadiness of the new skis this is no longer necessary. Also the average skier today is making tighter and more frequent turns and finds a shorter ski easier to handle. Skiers used to judge the length of a ski by reaching into the air and having the tip of the ski come to the break in the wrist. A good method now to measure the proper length of a ski is to reach the arm up and have the tip of the ski come halfway between the break in the wrist and the elbow. Of course, a top skier may want to use a somewhat longer ski because of his additional ability in handling it and his need for extra stability. However, even expert racers are using skis 5 cm. to 7 cm. shorter than they were ten years ago, especially in slalom and giant slalom competition.

Camber and Flex

Be careful not to choose a ski with too much camber. The camber should not exceed 1½″. The way to judge this is by putting the

2

running surfaces of the skis together with the tips and tails touching. The distance between the middle of the skis is the camber. Too much camber makes a ski difficult to turn. Most good skis today have from ¾″ to 1½″ of camber.

Also be sure that you do not choose a pair of skis which are too stiff for you. It is preferable for an average skier to have skis a bit on the soft side rather than on the stiff side. They will be easier to handle in all phases of skiing. You should have the right flex in your skis for your height and weight. A good method of determining this is by putting one hand on the middle of the ski and the other hand at the tip of the ski. With the tail of the ski against the wall or the side of your foot, bend the ski by pulling with the top hand while pushing with the other hand. When this pressure is applied the ski should bend in an even curve from the tip to the tail. If the ski is the right flex for you, you will be able to do this; if you cannot bend the ski, then it is probably too stiff for you.

Types of Skis

There are four types of alpine skis to choose from: a slalom ski, a giant slalom ski, a combination ski, and a downhill ski. A slalom ski is slightly narrower and stiffer through the front part of the ski than the others. This ski is used to advantage at moderate speed in very hard packed or icy conditions because of its manoeuvrability. A giant slalom ski is slightly wider and has a much softer tip. The reason for the softer tip is to allow a racer to run freer and faster when he is running straight in giant slalom races. The racer will usually use a slightly longer giant slalom ski than he does for slalom. This ski performs well in all types of turns except that it does not manoeuvre as quickly in tight turns as a slalom ski. It does, however, perform better at high speeds. The giant slalom skis of today are so well designed that they are suitable for almost any type of skier.

A combination or "combi" ski is similar to the giant slalom and also good for all around skiing. There is so little difference, in fact, that I believe you will see the term "combi" disappear in the near future. The downhill ski is wider than all of the other types; also longer, stiffer and stronger, with a very flexible tip. The extra stiffness and strength are to allow the skier to track at high speed, and the soft tip is to allow the skis to run freely in a straight line at high speed. The extra length is for stability and good tracking performance at high speed. A good skier can enjoy himself on a downhill ski if he is making long radius turns, but the disadvantage of this type of ski is the weight which is harder to handle and will tire a skier if he uses it all day. Either a very flexible downhill ski or a giant slalom ski of reasonable length would be suitable when skiing in deep powder.

Maintenance

Most good skis have a base of some type of polyethylene. By all means choose a ski with such a base because of its fine sliding qualities and lasting wear. It will seldom need waxing and if wax is necessary, these bases hold it very well. They are easy to maintain and can be easily repaired with Ptex candles or patches.

Today's skis usually have hidden edges—meaning that there are no screws showing at all. The only skis which have edges held on by screws that show are very inexpensive skis and should be avoided unless you really cannot afford anything else.

BOOTS

Materials

There are so many good boots on the market today that it is very difficult for most skiers to decide which is the one best for them. It is generally accepted that the new plastic buckle boots are preferable to leather, but there are many different types of these at varying prices and this creates a difficult decision for most people. Plastic boots are being manufactured in approximately three price ranges: moderate, moderately expensive, and expensive. There are excellent boots for all types of skiers in all price ranges. I would advise that you choose the brand which fits you best, in spite of any personal preferences for model, colour, or style. It is extremely important that every skier have a perfectly fitted boot.

Foam

A few years ago foam boots came onto the market as a means of perfecting the fit on the individual foot. Recently these boots have been improved to the point where they are gaining a great deal of popularity and are certainly advantageous when properly fitted. The methods of injecting the foam are much superior today to those used in the beginning and the foam itself has been perfected. Also ski shop employees have gained a great deal of experience with the foam boots and are now better able to give customers a good fit.

Of course, if you can get a good fit in a regular boot without being foamed, you may find one which suits you very well at less expense. If you have any difficulty, however, with your feet—if they are difficult to fit, are very sensitive to the cold, or if an old injury has left a slight malformation—it would certainly be worth your while to try foam. You will be more likely to get a perfect fit and you will probably find the boots warmer because of the insulation which the foam provides.

Fitting

How does a boot feel when it fits perfectly? Your foot should be in contact with the inner part of the boot so that you do not feel it moving around at *any* point. It is also important to have no play whatsoever in the fit of your heel. If your heel lifts to any extent the boot is too big for you. By having heel play you are losing control in your skiing and you are also more likely to get sore spots on your heels. However, a well fitted boot should not squeeze your toes from the side or from the top. Although your foot is in solid contact with the boot you should be able to wiggle your toes slightly. This is necessary for good circulation so that the feet do not become cold and cramped.

It is a good idea to try on a boot with just one thin sock. Some people who wish an exceptionally close fit are even fitted in bare feet. Most boots will give a little, and after skiing with them for some time you will find that you will be able to wear a heavier pair of socks and still have a close fit.

Other Features

Buckles are, of course, standard equipment on all modern boots. Lately there is a trend towards cutting down on the number of buckles—some boots have only two or three. The advantage, of course, is that the boots are easier and quicker to get into with no loss of support.

Recently there has been a great deal of popularity of the high back boot, mainly brought on by their use by racers. I personally believe the need has been exaggerated for the average skier and think you will see them cut down somewhat in the future. A high back gives an expert skier support when he wants to rock backwards on his skis for a split second, but I don't believe that this is at all necessary for an intermediate skier. A boot which is just slightly higher in the back will give the intermediate sufficient additional support in the event that he is caught leaning back or when he is skiing avalement, and will be more comfortable for him than the very high back. I have seen some skiers actually hindered in their skiing by leaning back all of the time, mainly because they were wearing "jet sticks" or had extremely high back boots and thought it "the thing to do." Actually, a good skier is forward on his skis most of the time. In fact, it is impossible to ski well leaning back all of the time.

BINDINGS

What to Buy

It is essential for all skiers to take advantage of the safety, or release, bindings which are available today. You are aware that a good, well fitted pair of boots is very important and this is certainly true, but it is just as important to invest a fair amount of your budget in a good release toe and heel binding. Almost any of the well-known higher priced bindings of this type are excellent. They are certainly worth the price and if they are properly lubricated and adjusted should function well for you at all times and last for many years. There are many quite inexpensive bindings on the market but most of the ones I have seen cannot compare in safety and durability with the more costly types which are actually precision equipment.

Adjusting and Mounting

It is most essential that you take your bindings to a reputable ski shop so that they can be properly adjusted by someone who knows the binding and how it functions, and can adjust it according to your height and weight. There are now good checking devices available to ski shops for testing bindings. For a small fee you can ascertain whether or not your binding adjustment is correct. Do not attempt to adjust your bindings yourself as, without experience in this area, it is almost impossible to judge the correct pressure needed to release them. It is just as important not to have the bindings too loose as it is not to have them too tight. Some of the top bindings have a great deal of elasticity before they release. Such bindings can be set somewhat more loosely than bindings without this characteristic. Most people have their bindings mounted at the ski shop. However, if you wish to do this yourself, here is an easy way to determine where the binding should be placed. With the ski flat on a table or on the floor, measure from the front of the tip to the tail—without allowing for the curve of the tip. Take one-half of this distance and draw a line across the ski. The tip of the sole of your boot should be on that line if you have an average sized foot. If your foot is very large (say a size 12 or 13) you can go ½″ to ¾″ ahead of this measurement.

POLES

Length

Most people are now using a somewhat shorter pole than before, mainly because of changes in skiing techniques. A good rule of thumb for length is to choose poles one to two inches shorter than three-quarters of your height. Another method is to choose poles which are approximately 3″ under your armpit when held under the arm with the tip on the floor. A pole should be of proper length because it will allow your body to be in a proper position when you are planting the pole for a turn. For good skiing it is important to have a light and well balanced pair of poles. This means that when you hold the pole by the handle, the bottom, or basket end, feels light and easy to use.

Balance and Strength

There are a number of medium priced poles available which are quite light and have a reasonably good balance. The more expensive poles usually have a bit better balance and because of better material used in the shaft are much stronger. They also usually have a much stronger basket. It is, of course, not necessary for the average skier to purchase a very expensive pair of poles as long as he is satisfied that they are well balanced and reasonably light. It is important, however, to choose a pole with a good handle and a strap which may be adjusted to any size of hand. Most good straps are still made of leather and after skiing for some time the leather will stretch and need adjusting. It will have to be shortened by adjusting the buckle to fit your hand.

CLOTHING AND ACCESSORIES

There is a great selection of attractive and warm ski clothing manufactured today, all of which is extremely suitable. The only advice I can offer in this respect is that you invest in a good pair of warmup pants, some warm underwear, and a good pair of gloves or mitts since it is virtually impossible to ski well when you are feeling cold.

You will need goggles for skiing on a snowy day and these will be used more and more in all weathers when your skiing improves and you are skiing faster. You can pick up a good pair for from $3 to $6 and any type which feels comfortable on your face is fine. Some people seem to find that a yellow lens is best for them and some prefer orange—this is really a matter of personal preference. A good pair of goggles will increase visibility in all conditions, especially when the light on a slope is "flat."

Advice To The Beginner

HOW TO GET STARTED

It is very important for a beginner to start off on the right foot. The first step, if at all possible, is to go to a reputable shop to be outfitted so that you can take advantage of the advice of professionals. If you can get some advice from a ski instructor as well, so much the better. Try to avoid taking advice from your friends or picking up second-hand equipment or equipment sold in "package deals" which hasn't been checked over by someone knowledgeable enough to detect any signs of warpage or wear or unsuitability to your height and weight. (Of course you may wish to rent equipment in the beginning but if you plan to continue you will want your own—particularly your own boots.)

Buying Equipment

There is a very wide choice in ski equipment today and most of it is very good. Prices can vary a great deal and this factor is sometimes very confusing to a beginner. While it is of course important to start out with good equipment it is not necessary to spend a great deal of money, since there are many lines of skis, boots and poles which are moderately priced and more than adequate for the novice. Many of the advantages inherent in the more expensive skis, boots and poles would be wasted on the beginner as he would be unable to use the costly characteristics to advantage. For example, a $250 pair of skis could actually hinder the advancement of a beginner as compared to a ski worth from $75 to $150. The reason for this is that the high performance of the very expensive ski is made especially for fast and hard skiing. It is therefore usually more difficult to handle and to turn for the skier who is just beginning to ski at low speeds. A ski of high calibre will cut and carve well under the feet of a very good skier but will not slide around easily for a skier in the first stages of learning to ski.

Of course, as previously mentioned, it is very important for all types of skiers to invest as much as possible in a good release binding. I would also suggest that while a good, firm boot is extremely necessary for the novice, this can be found among the more moderately priced line of any well-known make of boot on the market. A beginner or low intermediate certainly need not invest a great deal of money in a top competition boot.

Taking Lessons

When starting to ski, avoid having a friend try to teach you if he is not a trained instructor. This can turn out to be disappointing and discouraging and downright dangerous. Skiing is perhaps the one sport that is practically impossible to learn on your own because control is absolutely necessary for your safety and pleasure. If you really want to get started off on the right foot try to afford the time and money to spend a ski week at a resort known for its good instruction. A solid week of lessons is worth many, many weekends of hourly instruction. If a ski week is not possible, try to get in as many hours of lessons as possible on consecutive weekends so that there will be continuity in your instruction.

It is less expensive to take group lessons than private lessons and you will certainly benefit by them a great deal. However, if you can afford a private lesson now and then, you will find that you will progress more rapidly.

A Word of Caution

A beginner should, of course, have had his bindings adjusted by a professional, but it is also wise to have their function and characteristics explained to him. It is a good idea to have the bindings checked often to make certain that they have remained in the proper setting. You will need to know how to get in and out of your binding with ease should you fall and your skis come off on the hill, and you will need to know how the binding functions in case it is loosened while skiing or travelling. Sometimes a binding can loosen while on a car rack because of the vibrations. It is a good idea to carry your skis in some kind of a bag for protection, since corrosion from dust and chemicals on the roads can cause bindings to tighten up when travelling.

Choosing a Good Teaching Area

A beginner does not need to go to one of the largest, highest, and most expensive areas to obtain good ski lessons. Many of the smaller areas have excellent slopes for the purpose of teaching beginners and perhaps even more variety for them than some of the higher areas. It is, of course, important to choose one with a well established ski school but this can probably be found reasonably close to where you live. Choose an area with lots of wide, easy slopes which are used especially or specifically for teaching. There is much less chance of your feeling insecure or nervous in such an area when you are first starting out.

Short Skis

A great many beginners these days are taking advantage of the short or gradual length method. This is extremely helpful in the first stages of learning to ski. Shorter length skis give the beginner confidence because they are easier to handle and manoeuvre and make the first lessons easier for him. Some schools use several different lengths but we have had great success using first a 135 cm. and then a 170 cm. length and finally the length most suitable for the individual skier. The length, of course, can vary according to his height, weight and ability. Some people find that a 170 cm. ski is a very enjoyable length for them because they like to ski at moderate speed and they like the manoeuvrability of that length.

ADVICE TO INSTRUCTORS

In my own school I have found that it is extremely important for the confidence and advancement of the pupil to do a lot of straight running, traversing, and some climbing on skis before attempting to teach him how to turn. We are spending a considerable amount of time teaching people to ski straight down a hill and to traverse the hill and, while doing this, we teach them to stop by falling and sitting down properly. This seems to give them much needed confidence in these early stages of skiing because they feel secure in the knowledge that they know how to stop by falling properly. After the pupil has done a fair amount of straight running and traversing his running position and balance have improved to a great extent. He is now ready to go into making turns with confidence and has a greater ability to be free in his movements. The time spent in these early stages builds up a very gradual increase in speed so that the beginner does not feel any fear when he lets his skis run a little.

Before the straight running and traversing, the pupil is taught to walk for a few minutes and to slide. He is also taught to turn around both ways in a step turn. Following this he is taught to climb a hill in a side step. While he is climbing the hill he is often stopped by the instructor and checked for position to see that he is standing properly on the hill. The position the pupil is in at this point is a traverse position, and he has achieved this position without actually being aware of it. Climbing also teaches the pupil a great deal about edging, control of poles, and the manoeuvrability of his skis. After climbing the hill a number of times and then traversing and descending in a straight running position, the skier is ready for the snowplow and turns.

We have found that when this method is used in the beginning it makes a tremendous difference in the progress of the pupil when he is taught turns compared with teaching him a snowplow and snowplow turns from the beginning.

Let's Begin

CONDITIONING FOR BEGINNERS

With the emphasis these days on exercise and physical fitness, many people keep themselves in fairly good condition, and these people will naturally progress a great deal faster when learning to ski than those who have not kept themselves fit. It is a good idea, therefore, to do some pre-season exercising such as bicycling, running, climbing, or any action sport such as tennis or squash. However, if you have not had a chance to get into good condition before the beginning of the ski season, don't be discouraged if some of your friends progress faster than you do. You will, of course, gradually get into better shape just by skiing, but take it easy at first because you will naturally tire more quickly in the beginning.

CARRYING SKIS AND POLES

The best way to carry your skis, particularly if you are going any distance, is to have them tied together with safety straps or rubber ski bands. This is important because it will keep one edge from sliding over the other and damaging the edges. If you are travelling a short distance it is not necessary to hold the poles under the skis as in the pictures, but when travelling farther this helps to distribute the weight onto both shoulders and makes it less tiring.

With the skis tied together and one hand near the tips and the other near the middle, swing the skis over to the opposite shoulder. Now balance the skis with one hand while you lift the poles and place them under the skis as shown.

HOW TO HOLD POLES

There is only one way to hold a ski pole. The hand is reached up through the loop with the back of the strap over the front part of the wrist. The thumb and hand are closed over the strap and onto the handle of the pole. When the pole handle is grasped the top of the hand should be approximately ½″ from the top of the pole. Holding them in this manner will give you maximum control of your poles while skiing.

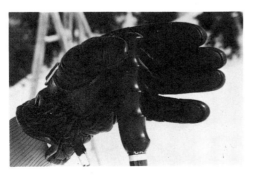

WALKING ON SKIS

Walking on skis is not too different from walking on foot, except that you will naturally want to slide forward as you step and so you will be covering more ground sliding than walking. Practising walking will give you the feeling of your skis and help your balance.

As the right ski slides ahead the opposite arm is brought forward and the pole is planted. Keep your weight on the forward ski while preparing to move the other ski forward.

The left ski is now brought forward and the opposite arm is moved ahead and the pole planted. The pole is used for balance and to help propel you ahead.

STEP TURN

After you have walked some distance in a straight line you will use a step turn to make your first turn on the flat. A step turn is one of the easiest and most comfortable methods for a beginner to turn around on skis. This can be done with the poles lifted off the snow to keep them out of the way when you are on the flat, but the use of poles will be necessary when turning on a hill.

Standing with skis parallel one pole is planted close to the tip of the ski and the other is planted to the side and at the rear of the opposite ski.

Raise the tip of one ski off the ground and move it away from the opposite ski while leaving the tail in the snow. Shift your weight to the ski you have just moved and bring the other ski parallel. In the beginning the width of the step should be small but as your ability increases the width is increased.

Repeat the step several times and you will be right back where you started.

SIDE STEP

The side step is the easiest and most practical way for a beginner to climb a hill. It is a step which will be widely used throughout all of your skiing. Even experts use it most of the time when climbing a steep hill. This step teaches you a great deal about edge control which is very important in all stages of skiing. When you are climbing a hill in a side step and come to a stop with the feet together, you are standing in a natural traverse position.

Plant the uphill pole at arm's reach directly away from your feet.

Step uphill with the uphill ski, edging it well into the snow. Shift your weight to the uphill ski.

Lift the downhill ski and bring it parallel to the uphill ski.

THE FIRST SLIDE

After climbing eight to ten steps up in the side step on a very gentle slope, you are ready to place your skis in a shallow traverse which will allow you to slide when your poles are lifted from the snow.

Assume the traverse position which you have already been shown while learning to climb. In a proper traverse position it is extremely important to have more weight on the downhill ski with knees slightly flexed, upper body erect, and arms carried low, relaxed and slightly forward.

Both poles are planted firmly in the snow at the tips of the skis and slightly to the side. With your weight supported by the poles, the tail of the uphill ski is lifted and placed on its uphill edge.

The downhill ski is brought parallel to the uphill ski and placed on its inside edge.

When the skis are parallel the poles are lifted from the snow and the skis begin to slide. Notice that the uphill ski is leading slightly and that the body is in a comfortable, relaxed position with knees slightly bent.

LEARNING TO FALL

When you have traversed the hill, it is then important to know how to stop by sitting down—or falling—properly.

From a traverse the hips are lowered and the skier sits back and into the uphill side of the hill.

As the body comes in contact with the snow the upper body leans back and both arms are spread out to each side. This results in the tips of the skis being raised off the snow.

To rise, the skis are swung around to a horizontal position across the slope below the body. With the feet drawn up close to the hips, push yourself up onto your feet with the aid of your arm or pole.

SECOND SLIDE

Running straight down the fall line should be practised on a gentle slope with a long, flat outrun. It should be long enough in comparison with the vertical drop of the hill to allow you to come to a gradual stop on your own. This is important in gaining full confidence in being able to stop when there are no obstacles in the way. At first a beginner should start part way up the hill and then gradually farther and farther up, increasing his speed all of the time. It is thrilling in the beginning to feel an increase of speed, and each time you will be more relaxed on your skis. This will enable you to learn the next steps in skiing far more easily than if you had not had this practice. Straight running is often neglected when a person is learning to ski and this can be a disadvantage to him later on.

A front view of a straight running position. The feet are apart with the weight evenly distributed on both skis. The body is erect with the hands held low, relaxed and slightly to the front. The knees are slightly bent and the skier looks straight ahead and not down at his skis.

Side view of straight running. Notice the position of the body and the slight bend in the knees.

HERRINGBONE

This is an effective method of climbing a short steep hill, but it would be too tiring to use for a climb of any length. The herringbone should be practised on flat or almost flat terrain at first and then on a smooth steeper slope. Holding the poles in the regular manner is fine if you are climbing a medium slope, but if you are climbing a steep slope it is better to place your hands on the top of the poles as this will give you more power and will be less tiring.

With skis in a "V" position, the left ski is picked up and placed on its inside edge.

The weight is transferred to the left ski and with the support of the poles the right ski is lifted forward onto its inside edge. The poles are used as an aid moving alternatively with the opposite leg and are kept behind and wide apart at all times. The step should be just long enough to keep the skis from crossing at the back.

KICK TURN

A kick turn is a very quick way of changing direction whether on a flat or on a hill, and it will be used often throughout your skiing. It can be used to great advantage when it is necessary to change direction on a narrow, steep hill. While it is possible to do this turn either uphill or downhill, I would recommend a downhill kick when you are on a slope because it is easier and safer.

With all of the weight on the uphill ski, kick the downhill ski forward and up on its heel. Support your balance with poles and arms.

Keeping the tail on the snow, swing the tip of the downhill ski around and down parallel to the uphill ski.

Shift the weight to the downhill ski while bringing the unweighted ski around and parallel. The uphill pole follows.

23

SKIING BUMPS

Sometimes while you are skiing you will be running straight over moguls or diagonally crossing a hill which is full of moguls. This type of descent often frightens people, but if skied properly it can be fun and also excellent practice in timing. It is very important to be supple and relaxed in this type of skiing.

When entering a hollow on the downhill side of a bump, the knees are flexed; the body is quite erect and slightly forward.

As you start up the other side of the next bump the body begins to lower with a flexion of the knees and hips. The hands are kept forward.

When the crest of the bump is reached, the body is in a very low position and the weight is moved forward with arms carried low and to the front. This low and forward position will allow the tips to drop over the bump and remain in contact with the snow.

Descending on the opposite side, the body returns to a more erect position.

SKATING

As the skier is returning across the flat to the bottom of the slope he can be taught skating which is excellent for balance, coordination, weight transfer, and edge control. These four things are the key to good skiing.

Skating on skis is similar to skating on ice skates. Place one ski in a "V" on its outside edge. As you push off, the back foot is lifted and you glide onto the forward ski.

Before the glide comes to a stop the back foot is brought forward close to the gliding ski. It is then placed in the snow in a "V" position and on its outside edge.

With a thrust of the opposite foot glide again on the forward ski. Notice how the arms should swing from side to side with each skating step.

SNOWPLOW TURNS

You are now ready to learn to change direction in the snow while moving, by using a slowplow turn. This turn is important because it helps you to understand the mechanics of a turn, the correct body position over the skis, and how to control your speed. At this point you also learn what it means to steer the skis with your legs. This steering with the legs is used in all skiing turns and is therefore important to learn correctly at this point.

The snowplow is also used as a good braking manoeuvre, but in the sequence it is shown more as a gliding turn than a braking turn. The skis are flatter than they would be if the turn was used for braking. A ski will turn easily if it is weighted and steered because the tip—or shovel—is wider than the waist of the ski.

The turn is started from a traverse position.

After gaining momentum in a traverse position the uphill ski is either lifted or slid into a snowplow position, the weight is transferred to the stemmed ski, and steering begins with the outside leg.

28

While the steering is taking place it is important to have the legs equally bent. This will keep the inside ski flat and allow the skis to come around easily.

Upon completion of the turn notice how square the body is in relation to the skis and how both knees are bent. The arms are carried away from the body and moved naturally in a circular motion with the turn.

UPHILL CHRISTIE

Straight side slipping down a hill may be taught before this exercise, but if the sequence up to now has been followed closely it is not usually necessary. It is very important in this exercise to have the skis as flat on the snow as possible when the lower ski is slid out into a stem position because it is used more to glide than to brake.

From a slight downhill traverse position the lower ski is slid into a downhill stem. The body is centred and the inside edge of the lower ski released allowing the ski to slip across the snow.

During the side slip of the downhill ski, the tail of the uphill ski is picked up and brought parallel to the downhill ski. The weight is concentrated on the downhill ski. Notice the angle of the uphill leg as the ski is being picked up. When the uphill ski is returned to the snow it is placed slightly on its uphill edge.

While the skis are sliding forward and sideways the feet are slightly apart and the uphill ski is leading. When the skis are brought even during this exercise, it is an open stance with the skis slightly apart and the weight directly over both skis. It should be practised from both directions. Once you can sideslip your skis from either side you are ready to go on to the christie progression.

CHRISTIE PROGRESSION

In the christie progression there are four stages as illustrated in the following sequences. As you progress, the skis are closed to a parallel position before the fall line instead of after crossing the fall line. The pole is not used in the first two stages because I believe that if the skier is taught to use the pole plant as a pivot, he soon tends to rely on it too much. The result is a square and jerky turn.

Stage One

From a traverse position the uphill ski is lifted into a stem position. With a steering action of the legs the skis will seek the fall line.

As the downhill ski crosses the fall line it assumes most of the weight. The tail of the uphill ski is picked up and brought parallel to the downhill ski and placed on its uphill edge.

With continued steering the turn will
be completed.

Stage Two

This turn is started as in Stage One.

When the outside ski is pointing straight down the fall line the inside ski is picked up and brought parallel.

A strong steering action of the legs will keep the skis turning into the new direction.

Notice the angle of the inside leg. The knee is pointing slightly uphill. It is extremely important that the knee not be tilted inward because it will cause the inside edge of the ski to cut into the snow and completely block your turn.

Stage Three

In Stage Three the speed has increased and the downhill ski is lifted and brought parallel well before entering the fall line. As it is lifted, there is a pronounced forward transfer of weight. At this stage the pole is planted, to be used as a pivot for the turn.

As the uphill ski is stemmed, it is placed slightly on its inside edge. At the same time the pole is planted as the body is lowered.

As the body rises the weight is transferred forward onto the uphill ski and the tail of the downhill ski is picked up and brought parallel. (The tip of the ski remains on the snow to ensure the forward transfer of weight and to simplify the edge change of that ski.)

With a steering action of the legs and feet the skis begin turning. Continued steering action will complete the turn.

(Note that the skis are parallel with a slightly open stance before entering the fall line. As the skier improves and speed is increased the width of the stem is cut down narrower and narrower.)

Stage Four (Step Christie)

When you have thoroughly practised Stages One, Two, and Three of the *Christie Progression*, you are ready for more advanced christies. Once speed has been built up, it is easier to step the uphill ski out parallel than to stem it out into a half snowplow position at the beginning of the turn. We call this a "step christie" or an "open stance christie." When executing a step christie at moderate speed, the pole plant may be used but is not necessary (except perhaps when doing short radius turns). Personally I find this type of turn easier to do without planting the pole although the action of the arm and pole is the same.

From a traverse the uphill ski is stepped out parallel or almost parallel to a comfortable width. The width of the opening depends upon your speed—the greater the speed the smaller the opening should be.

With a slight up motion and transfer of weight to the uphill ski, the downhill ski is picked up and brought parallel. The moment the weight is transferred to the uphill ski steering action of the legs begins.

Continued steering action will complete the turn. The arms are carried low and the outside arm follows the curve of the turn.

Getting Into Parallel

INTRODUCTION TO PARALLEL

There are a couple of exercises which can be used with a great deal of success and which are very important aids to parallel skiing. The first is what we call "flexion-extension" without the use of the poles. The second is similar except that each time the body flexes the pole is planted. Both these exercises should be practised on the flattest hill possible. In fact a hill of only a few degrees is adequate as long as you can slide at all. If too steep a hill is chosen it is difficult to get the correct timing of the pole action because the skis are sliding too quickly.

FLEXION-EXTENSION

Both front and side views are given to show the erect and low positions in this exercise.

Assume a straight running position with a slightly open stance.

After sliding some distance lower your body from the knees and hips.

Rise again to a normal straight running position.

The body is lowered again as before. This lowering of the body should be easy and relaxed and not hurried.

FLEXION-EXTENSION WITH POLE ACTION

Assume a straight running position—again with feet slightly apart.

The body lowers and at the same time the pole is brought forward and planted halfway between the tip of the ski and the boot. The body rises again before the pole is released from the snow and pointed towards the rear. As the body is lowered again the opposite pole is brought forward and planted.

(After the exercise has been practised, it can be repeated with a retraction of the skis on the up motion and with a slight change of direction.)

BODY POSITIONS

There are four basic body positions in relation to weight distribution over the skis. Each one is used at certain times in skiing depending upon the type of turns you are executing and the type of terrain that is involved. In all of the pictures I have used a ski pole to illustrate the weight distribution.

In a normal stance the skier is in a well-balanced position (if his binding placement is correct).

With more ankle bend the body moves forward shifting the weight to the front of the skis. This is usually called a "forward transfer."

The extreme backward position is used when skiing avalement or when the feet are projected forward. The body is moved farther back and more into a sitting position which shifts the weight entirely onto the tails of the skis. A slightly higher back boot is a great aid in maintaining this position.

Taken from action the three body positions appear as illustrated:

The normal skiing stance: weight is directly over both skis.

The forward position: shown in course of completing a turn, weight is forward to round out the turn.

Example of avalement: notice the position of the body in comparison to the preceding sequence. The turn is started with the weight on the tails of the skis.

PARALLEL CHRISTIE WITH UP-UNWEIGHTING

In the parallel christie the body is in a very similar position to what it was in the preceding exercises. The flexion-extension (or "down-up-down" motion) is very important. The up motion will lighten the skis, change the edges, and help the skis to start turning in the new direction. While it is easier to make a parallel turn starting close to the fall line, I am showing it here more from a traverse as in linked parallel turns in order to give a clearer picture of the manoeuvre.

From a traverse position the body is lowered and the pole is planted approximately halfway between the tip of the ski and the toe of the boot.

As the body is extended from the knees and hips, the skis are lightened and the weight is transferred to the outside ski.

With the aid of the pole and the steering action of the legs, the skis are moved laterally across the hill into the new direction.

With a down pressure of the knees the edges begin to bite into the snow to help carve the turn. The majority of the weight remains on the downhill ski.

At the end of the turn the body is in a position to lower again and start a turn in the opposite direction.

Parallel Garlands

Parallel garlands are a series of parallel turns done diagonally across the hill. They are a great aid to skiing parallel because they teach timing, rhythm and changing of edges. They are often used by good skiers during a run for variety and additional rhythm.

From a traverse position the skis are moved across the hill. When a fair amount of momentum has been obtained the skis are turned uphill.

At the end of the uphill turn the downhill pole is planted and the skis are turned downhill.

As the skis cross the fall line the inside pole is planted and the skis are turned uphill again.

47

HOP CHRISTIE (AIRPLANE TURN)

A hop christie, or "airplane turn" as it is sometimes called, is fun to do and is a very quick method of changing direction. It is used often throughout your skiing, especially in bumpy terrain where it can be used to clear a considerable amount of distance over more than one bump or other obstables. When using hop christies remember to absorb shock upon landing by lowering the body slightly.

In preparation for the lift the body is well lowered and the pole is planted.

As the body rises the knees are drawn up, and the skis are jumped off the snow and turned slightly into the new direction.

Upon landing the legs are slightly bent at the knees to absorb shock, and the skis are on the inside edges.

A forward steering action of the legs keeps the skis turning.

ADVANCED AIRPLANE TURNS

After the hop christie has been practised you may want to try a more advanced type of airplane turn. More speed and height will be necessary which means that you will cover more distance. This type of turn may be used going over a single bump of large or medium height, or it may be used to take off from one bump clearing two or three others while turning in the air.

In the following sequence I have shown an advanced airborne turn over a series of small bumps.

With the aid of the upshoot from the bump and with a strong spring in the legs, the skis become airborne. The body is held forward slightly for balance. The pole may or may not be used depending upon your speed. It is usually not used at very high speed.

The arms are held low and well forward, the knees are drawn up (close to the body), and the tips of the skis are dropped following the contour of the slope.

The legs are extended and the arms are drawn up slightly in preparation to absorb shock upon landing. Notice that the skis have changed direction while airborne.

Skiing With The Experts

SKI WITH FLARE

Many skiers rest on their laurels once they can ski parallel fairly well and seem to feel that further lessons are not necessary, or that advanced skiing is only for the special few. This is not at all true; any good parallel skier can learn all of these advanced turns and so refine his technique that he can ski well on any type of terrain or snow condition. He will experience the excitement of skiing with grace and confidence down a steep, bumpy hill, or clearing with ease a series of bumps and hollows. He will never again avoid a difficult slope because of lack of confidence in his ability to handle it.

LONG RADIUS CARVED TURNS

Long radius parallel turns are generally used when skiing an open slope which is not too steep. It is, of course, possible to ski a steep slope with long radius turns but the speed would be too great for most skiers. In these long turns the extension of the body at the beginning of the turn is somewhat exaggerated and the down motion throughout the turn is very gradual.

At the end of one turn the body is lowered and the pole is planted. Note the position of the upper body in relation to the hips.

The body rises from the knees and the weight is transferred to the outside ski. With a steering action of the legs the skis begin to turn, and the planted pole is released from the snow.

Continued steering action completes the turn. Note how the arms are moving in a circular motion to the outside and the body is well forward.

Also, notice the position of the hips in relation to the legs as the turn is completed.

SHORT RADIUS TURNS WITH UP-UNWEIGHTING

Short radius turns can be used on almost any type of terrain. A good rhythm can be built up and maintained when these turns are linked quickly. The skis should be turned sharply and completely out of the fall line before the next turn is attempted. To keep your speed to a minimum when skiing a steep slope, the skis should be turned even more sharply. The forward transfer of weight is very important and this is achieved by bending the knees more during the steering action.

At the end of one turn the pole is planted and the body is facing downhill with knees flexed (a good example of anticipation).

As the body rises the weight is quickly transferred to the outside, the edges are changed, and the skis are quickly steered into the new direction.

With knees well bent and weight forward, the skis are sharply turned. Notice the position of the hips and upper body and the strong forward knee drive, causing the edges to bite and carve a good turn.

At the end of the turn the pole is planted, the body rises, and the weight is again transferred to the outside ski, ready for the next turn.

WEDELN

Wedeln is really a series of linked parallel turns with a slight setting of the edges before each turn. It is important not to hesitate between one turn and the next. The slight setting of the edges before each turn develops rhythm. In wedeln the upper body is always facing somewhat downhill; the steeper the slope the more downhill it will face. The timing and placement of the pole plant is very important when skiing wedeln. On intermediate slopes the pole is usually planted about three-quarters of the way up to the tip of your skis and close to a foot (or less) to the side. On a steeper slope the pole should be planted a bit farther back and slightly more to the side. It is very important never to be sitting back during the edge set. The up and down movement (flexion-extension) is minimal and quick, and the knees are always pressed forward.

When the skis cross the fall line, the pole is planted and the edges are lightly set.

With a slight up motion and forward transfer of weight, and with the aid of the pole, the skis begin to turn.

With weight still forward a down pressure of the knees will cause the skis to carve sharply.

As the skis cross the fall line again the pole is again planted, edges are set, and the next turn has begun.

Notice the angulation of the body while the skis are crossing the fall line. This causes the skis to edge sharply and minimizes side slipping.

LIGHT EDGE SET WITH DOWN UNWEIGHTING

In this sequence the edge check is not as strong or as powerful as in the preceding sequences because I am skiing on a somewhat flatter hill. (The edge check would be stronger if I were again on a steep hill.) In this turn the skis are unweighted by a sudden lowering of the hips which is opposite to the up-unweighting motion shown before. It is, in fact, an exaggerated avalement. This turn is more often used at slow-to-moderate speeds over bumps or sudden drop-offs. The skis remain in contact with the snow at all times.

The edges are set and the pole is planted. The upper body faces slightly downhill.

During the pole plant the hips are suddenly dropped to a low position. With the weight on the rear of the skis they are pivoted by a steering action of the legs into the new direction with the aid of a prolonged pole plant.

While the skis are turning the hips are raised slightly.

The hips are now in a normal position and the body is slightly angulated. The outside arm is moving forward in a circular motion to the outside.

At the end of the turn the body has returned to the almost erect, normally flexed position.

EDGE CHECK AND REBOUND OVER BUMPS

When skiing in bumpy terrain and using edge set to reduce speed and enhance control, it is necessary at times to take advantage of the rebound from the edge set and lift the tails of the skis off the ground to jump over the crest of the bump. This is especially true if the bump is sharp. The important thing to remember while using this type of lift is that the lifting action of the skis must be quick and you must be careful not to be caught leaning back upon take-off.

As the edges are set the pole is moved forward and planted, and with an extension of the knees the skis are picked up.

As the skis are clearing the crest of the bump the tips are dropped to follow the contour of the slope.

Upon landing the knees are slightly bent ready to absorb shock. It is important to be over the centre of your skis or even slightly forward when landing in order not to lose balance.

This is a good shot of an edge set— showing pole plant, edge set and anticipation.

AVALEMENT OVER A SMALL BUMP

The word *avalement* is derived from the French verb *avaler* which means "to swallow." The term "compression turn" is often used instead of *avalement* because it is the closest English translation of the meaning of the term. It refers to the fact that the skis are always in maximum contact with the snow when a turn is being made.

Avalement may be used to advantage while skiing through bumps. It is also used a great deal in competitive skiing—mostly in slalom. This turn was originally developed by racers and was made possible by the new higher backed boots which allow the skier to sit back and let his skis project from under him without losing balance.

When approaching a bump the skis are turned sharply so that they are at right angles to the fall line.

The body assumes a sitting position as the pole is planted. With the upper body facing downhill and with the aid of the pole and steering action of the legs, the skis begin to turn over the crest of the bump.

When the skis cross the fall line the hips rise and the knees are pushed forward to resume a normal forward position.

In the rear view of *avalement,* notice how the skis start at a right angle to the slope and how the upper body is facing downhill with the outside arm projecting towards the new direction.

SKIING A STEEP SLOPE

It is, of course, more difficult to ski well on a steep slope than on a relatively flat one. The main reason is that you cannot afford to be caught with your weight back or on the up-hill ski of the turn. From the end of one turn to the beginning of the next your movements must be precise and quick.

When skiing on a steep hill the body position will always be more angulated than when skiing on a flat hill, and the weight will be more forward. At the end of a turn when the edges are set both skis are jumped laterally to the side and close to, or in, the fall line without any hesitation. The inside ski is held higher off the ground to enable the outside ski to assume all of the weight when it comes in contact with the snow. As the fall line is crossed the inside ski is lowered back onto the snow. Throughout the turn both arms are always forward. This turn is commonly used in competition when skiing through gates on an especially steep hill.

Crossing the fall line at the end of a turn the body is low and well angulated. The edges are set and the pole is planted.

With the aid of the pole plant, the body is slightly extended and the skis are jumped laterally to the side onto the new edges.

As the outside ski comes in contact with the snow, there is a strong steering action of the outside leg and a forward movement of the body.

The uphill ski is returned to the snow as the fall line is crossed.

This is the same turn but shown at a different angle and on a more moderately steep slope.

In the second picture note the solid pole plant to aid in moving the skis to the side and in the third picture notice the strong steering action of the downhill leg.

REBOUND TURNS WITH STRONG EDGE CHECK

A strong edge set is generally used when skiing steep hills because it can be used to check speed and allow you to maintain control. The important thing to remember when using strong edge set and rebound is to bring the skis completely across the hill when setting the edges. This is what holds your speed down.

As the edges are set the pole is planted and the upper body is facing downhill.

With the aid of the pole plant and the rebound the skis are moved laterally to the other side and the edges are changed. The tail of the inside ski is lifted and the weight is quickly transferred to the outside ski.

A steering action of the outside leg will quickly turn the skis. The tip of the inside ski is slightly tilted onto its inside edge. This will increase the turning power.

As the turn progresses the inside ski is returned to the snow parallel to the outside ski. The weight is still mostly on the outside ski.

The rear view of the same turn shows the weight distribution and body position.

Notice the way the body is facing downhill (angulation) while the pole is being planted, and how the outside arm projects forward.

In the second and third frames note the position of the skis and the forward transfer of weight.

ANTICIPATION

The term "anticipation" has been used rather loosely by skiers who do not really seem to understand the term. Actually all it means is that between the finishing of one turn and the beginning of the next, the outside arm leads the upper body as it twists and faces downhill to anticipate the new turn as the pole is planted. Anticipation is most apparent when skiing on a steep hill or in bumps, as the edges are set just before the turn takes place.

Front and rear view of anticipation on a steep hill: with a forward movement of the outside arm, the body faces downhill in anticipation of the next turn.

73

JUMPING OVER ONE OR MORE LARGE BUMPS

At times you will run into a series of large bumps and it is often easier to jump from one to another—or over a number—than it is to try to ride them all. Jumping over large moguls is not only necessary at times but it can be thrilling and fun.

The following sequence shows jumping from one large bump to the downhill side of another. In the same manner it is possible to clear more than one bump if they are not too far apart. Jumping over large bumps takes good judgment and pre-requires considerable practice on smaller bumps.

Approaching the crest of the first bump the body lowers and the hands are carried well forward.

At the crest of the bump the body is extended forward and the skis are jumped off the snow to gain height.

The skis are drawn up close to the body and the tips are dropped slightly to follow the contour of the ground.

Upon reaching the downhill side of the next bump the legs are extended and the tips are dropped farther so that the skis are parallel to the snow upon landing.

Upon landing the shock is absorbed by a slight lowering of the hips and knees.

AIRBORNE POSITIONS

In downhill skiing the skier is often airborne whether he wants to be or not. It is important to keep a crouched position in the air to maintain speed and in order to be in a proper position for landing. If you are in a low position when approaching the bump, this position should be maintained when you are airborne although it will be necessary to raise your body to a high position just before landing in order to absorb shock. As the body absorbs shock a low or medium position is resumed, depending upon the terrain ahead.

A jump is approached at high speed in a low crouch.

With skis parallel to the ground the body remains in the same position as much as possible.

Just before landing the body rises to a high position to cushion the landing and absorb shock.

Upon landing the body quickly returns to a medium position because of the rough terrain ahead.

Upon entering the bump, the terrain is extremely rough and therefore the poles are held down and to the side for balance instead of under the arms. The skis are parallel to the ground.

Going over the crest onto the steep part of the hill the tips of the skis are dropped to follow the contour of the hill in preparation for landing.

In a similar type of jump over a bump onto a steep hill when the terrain is smooth, you should stay more in a crouch and keep the poles under the arms.

A front view of the same jump shows the position of the body and skis. Notice how the tips of the skis are raised upon take off.

As maximum height is gained note the angle of the skis and the position of the body.

Just before landing the body extends ready to absorb shock.

SKIING ON ICE

To ski well on ice there are a few absolute essentials: you must have razor sharp edges and good skis with lots of life in them. You also need a good pair of boots with strong support and a sharp point on your ski poles. If the spike of your pole slips during the pole plant while skiing on ice the result will probably be a missed turn. If a fair amount of skiing has been done on icy conditions the spike on a pole will wear and become dull fairly quickly. It only takes a few seconds to have your tips sharpened in a ski shop on a grindstone or you can do the job yourself with a file.

When skiing on ice remember that your edge set must be firm and precise. Immediately afterwards, your weight must be transferred to the front of the skis quickly and smoothly. Good knee action and strong steering action with the legs will carve a good turn. Angulation is also important to keep the skis from side slipping. The amount of angulation used depends a great deal upon the radius of the turn, the speed you are skiing and the steepness of the slope. It will be most pronounced during the latter part of the turn.

It is also important to get off to a good start. Too much speed is not advisable when setting the edges in preparation for the first turn. If the first turn is properly executed you will be able to maintain a good rhythm throughout the run. However, if your first turn is missed it will be very hard to build up any rhythm because of the difficulty of recovering on ice.

One of the things that makes people nervous when skiing on ice is the extra noise created by vibrating or chattering skis. Since a well carved turn is quieter than a sliding turn, it is a good idea to practise on ice on a slope which is easy for you and not too steep. When straight running on icy conditions, it helps to turn both of your skis inward onto their inside edges. This will keep your skis tracking straight.

The following sequence shows two turns on ice on a medium slope.

During the pole plant the body is angulated and the edges are set.

With a slight extension of the legs the weight is transferred forward and the turn begins.

At the end of the turn the edges are set again and the pole is planted. The body is facing slightly downhill.

Again the body moves forward.

During the last part of the turn the body is angulated and the knees are well forward carving a true turn.

This is a good example of skiing on ice over a slight bump. It shows the edges cutting into the ice, good knee drive, and proper body position.

SKIING DEEP POWDER

Deep powder skiing can be tremendously enjoyable and thrilling, and is the dream of every skier. However, it is only enjoyable when skied with ability. It takes only six to eight inches of new snow to inhibit some people because, since they cannot see their skis, they seem to feel they will not be able to do anything with them.

The first rule to remember when skiing in deep snow is to have your weight as equally distributed on both skis as possible, especially at the beginning of a turn. Uneven weight distribution is the main cause of difficulty in this type of skiing. As the skis cross the fall line you will automatically carry more weight on the downhill ski but the uphill ski should still carry enough weight to keep it from floating up in the snow and turning uphill.

All movements should be quiet and fluid. When skiing in deep snow most people use a "down-up-down" or flexion-extension motion. This is probably the easiest method for an intermediate to learn and it is very effective. However, many skiers make the mistake of over-exaggerating their flexion-extension because of the fear that the tips of the skis will not come to the surface of the snow to start the turn. This can cause a lack of balance which may result in one ski sinking into the snow more than the other and will cause difficulty at the beginning of the turn.

When flexion-extension is used it can be minimal and still allow you to bring your ski tips to the top of the snow if most of your weight is carried towards the rear of the skis. When the skis rise to the top of the snow and begin turning, the forward transfer of weight should be gentle and easy. In other words, your knee action and forward bend at the waist should not be exaggerated.

Although deep snow can be handled well by good skiers using flexion-extension, it is even more advantageous for them to use avalement. The reason for this is that when using avalement there are fewer movements than when using flexion-extension, and the natural position of the body when using avalement will bring the tips of the skis to the surface of the snow automatically.

The basic movements used when skiing avalement are fundamentally the same whether you are skiing long radius turns, short radius turns, or tight turns with edge set on a steep hill. Because of these advantages avalement is being taught more and more to intermediates, particularly since the arrival of today's higher-back boots.

If you have never skied in deep snow before and you have an opportunity to do so, be sure to choose a slope which you would find easy to ski down on packed snow. For your first attempt try just two turns and give yourself plenty of room and time for them. Concentrate on having both skis weighted when you are preparing for the turn, and remember the points made here. With a little practice you'll know the real joy of skiing powder.

Ready For Competition

MODERN RACING

The following sequences are included not just for those who intend to do a great deal of serious racing, but also for those who will be in the odd fun race against friends or the ski school class. Racing can be fun in itself, but it can also improve your technique and judgment, speed up your reflexes, and improve your timing.

Any average skier in fairly good physical condition can learn these racing techniques although most people seem to feel that they are only for professional racers. When a person has learned to do them he certainly has an advantage over a skier who has not tried, whether skiing in competition or simply skiing for pleasure.

DOWNHILL POSITIONS

The three basic positions used by racers in downhill skiing are the low crouch, the medium crouch, and the high crouch. In all three crouches the feet should be apart approximately the width of the hips. Of course, this can vary slightly in accordance with the preference of the individual racer. Good crouching is very important in downhill racing, and judgment as to where and when to use the various types of crouches is probably the greatest asset a downhill skier can have.

In a low crouch the wind resistance is less than in a medium crouch and considerably less than in a high crouch. Therefore, you would naturally gain more speed in a low crouch; but when entering rough terrain a medium crouch is preferable because your skis will be more stable, and your knees and hips will be in a better position to absorb the variations in the terrain. Also, should you happen to catch an edge, you will have a better chance to recover if in this position.

A high crouch is used in extremely rough and steep terrain. In such terrain it might be necessary for you to drop your hands low and to the side for added balance. It is a mistake to try to hold a full crouch when the terrain is very rough because your body will take a great deal of pounding, and your skis will not ride as well as they would in a medium crouch. Although you will encounter more wind resistance in a medium crouch, the compensation over rough ground will be increased control of your skis, good tracking, and maximum speed for the terrain.

If you are not racing, you might find it advantageous at times to use a medium crouch to cross flats or "cat walks," or when *schussing* a hill which you are sure you can handle. A medium crouch will give you more stability, and since speed is not of the essence, a low crouch is unnecessary. A low crouch is very tiring and difficult to maintain if you are not in excellent condition. It is important in all three crouches not to have any forward bend in the ankles. Many skiers make this mistake and it results in too much weight on the front of the skis and lessens ability to absorb variation.

A side view of the low crouch: notice the angle of the thighs in relation to the skis, and how the upper body is partially suspended between the legs. The elbows are held in front of the knees and the hands are forward. The low crouch is sometimes referred to as an "egg position," the reason being apparent.

A side view of the medium crouch: the hips and upper body are carried higher, and the upper body is no longer suspended between the legs. The arms are held in the same manner except, of course, they are higher.

A side view of the high crouch: it is very similar to the medium crouch except that the hips, upper body, and arms are carried even higher.

A front view of the medium crouch: in all three types of crouches the head is held up so that you can see the terrain ahead.

MODERN RACING TURNS

When skiing in competition, the skis are often apart and at times in a "V" position, at the end of a turn. This "V" position is called a "skate turn" and is used to allow the skier to accelerate onto his uphill ski to gain height or a better line. This step up is sometimes used with avalement, but just as often with extension and forward transfer.

Generally speaking, in a long radius turn, extension and forward transfer of weight would be used. The pole is sometimes used, but the turn can also be executed without the pole. Whether or not the pole is used depends largely upon the type of terrain, the radius of the turn, and the speed involved. The step up with avalement is generally used for shorter and sharper radius turns. These are advanced turns and therefore it is extremely important that the skier be in excellent condition.

When moving at a fairly high speed it is difficult to transfer and project the weight to the uphill ski and a great deal of leg power is required for this purpose. The quicker the steering action begins with the uphill leg (once the weight has been projected to the uphill ski), the sooner the turn will be started.

SKATE TURN WITH PRONOUNCED "V"

Finishing a turn the body is angulated, resulting in stronger edging.

The body is projected uphill and the weight is transferred onto the uphill ski.

The uphill leg is extended and with a forward transfer of weight, accompanied by a strong steering action, the ski will begin to turn. The planting of the pole at this point is an additional aid in starting the turn.

The downhill ski is picked up and brought parallel.

Here is the same turn through gates.
In the first picture notice the angulation
of the body while coming around a gate.

The inside arm is tucked in close to the
body allowing the body to come close to
the flag.

Notice the forward projection of the body onto the uphill ski.

Note the forward lean of the body as the downhill ski is picked up.

SKATE TURN WITH A NARROWER "V"

Sometimes in competition an extremely high line is not necessary. This depends upon the gate combinations. If only moderate height must be gained, a similar turn is used except that the splitting of the skis into a "V" is less pronounced. Some split is still necessary, however, in order to accelerate and gain more speed. (If there is no height to be gained between gates, a normal parallel turn may be used, depending upon the skier's preference.)

This sequence is very similar to the preceding except that the skis are in a wide stance with just a slight "V."

The same sequence through gates showing slight split.

REFLEX TURN

In certain combinations of gates the skier does not have time to execute a skate turn even though some height may be necessary for a better line. Therefore, it is sometimes advantageous to lift the uphill ski and jump it over onto its new edge, or onto a flat ski (depending upon the terrain and the oncoming combination). It is jumped onto its new edge when a new turn must be initiated quickly in a tight combination. It is jumped onto a flat ski when the combination is not as tight and the turn does not have to be executed quite as quickly. The ski is then steered onto its new edge.

This manoeuvre is often used by racers, especially in slalom, without conscious thought and results from fine conditioning and quick reflexes.

This sequence shows jumping the uphill ski over onto its new edge in a tight combination.

As the gate is approached the body is in a forward position, and there is a strong steering action of the legs resulting in a sharply carved turn. Notice the way the inside arm is brought forward to follow the curve of the inside leg, allowing the body to come close to the gate.

Passing the gate, the inside arm is projected outwards and forward while the inside, or uphill, ski is lifted and moved to the side. With a strong spring off the edge of the downhill ski as it continues to run, the uphill lifted ski is turned slightly into the new direction and landed on its side edge. The downhill ski is lifted and is brought parallel. During this movement notice the avalement position and the forward projection of the skis.

The uphill ski lands on its inside edge, and with a forward transfer of weight and a strong steering action of the leg continues to turn in the new direction. The tip of the downhill ski is on the snow while the tail is slightly off the snow. This is important since it ensures that at this point the weight will be carried entirely on the turning ski. Also, the tip on the snow aids the steering action of the turn (sometimes referred to as "tip pull").

AVALEMENT IN A TIGHT TURN

When avalement is used at the right times, whether with split or parallel skis, it can be a very fast turn because edge set can be minimal or non-existent. This means that the skis will slide well and freely, keeping speed to a maximum. Avalement is used to advantage when you are carving a sharp turn and do not want to slow yourself down by holding too much on your edges. It is a turn used widely in competition today.

In this turn I am showing a slight split of the skis to gain height but I am using avalement to execute the turn instead of extension.

Passing a gate the skis are split slightly to gain height; the body is angulated and the inside arm is held close. The pole is moved forward to be planted.

With the body facing downhill the hips are quickly dropped to a sitting position causing the skis to project forward. With the aid of a prolonged pole plant and steering of the legs the turn is started.

96

The body extends slightly as the steering action of the legs continues strongly into the new direction.

Notice the angulation of the body as the gate is approached, and the forward position over the skis.

RUNNING A FLUSH WITH AVALEMENT AND WITH UP-UNWEIGHTING (EXTENSION)

It is quicker to run a flush using avalement than it is to run the same flush with up-unweighting. It can, however, be a bit trickier because, with the minimum edge hold, there is more chance of losing control of the skis. With practice and good physical condition, however, the benefits of avalement are obvious. While you will not gain as much speed using up-unweighting it may be necessary if the flush is set on a steep section of the hill.

Flush with Avalement

Flush with Up-Unweighting

At the beginning of each turn compare the position of the body.

Notice how much higher the hips are and how much more erect the body is at the beginning of the turn when using up-unweighting.

In avalement the hips are close to a sitting position at all times.

HIGH SPEED TURN

In high speed skiing it is very important to have the feet apart and the body well forward. There is more stability with the feet apart because each leg can work independently. Skiing at high speed with the feet locked together can be dangerous because there is less time to recover if you should hook an edge. Arms are held forward and to the side to help balance.

This is a high speed turn on hard surface. The body is well angulated to help the edges hold on the ice. Notice how the hips are leaning into the hill while the upper body is leaning out, and how the edges of both skis are carving and not slipping. Notice also how the inside ski is well advanced. This will prevent the skis from crossing because of the vibration and chatter which may occur at high speed.

This is a high speed turn on a softer, packed surface. The angulation of the body is less pronounced because the edges have a better chance to hold on softer snow.

Part Two
Cross Country Skiing

Cross Country Skiing

INTRODUCTION

In recent years cross country skiing has regained a great deal of popularity and, therefore, I have included some basic instruction for those who have never tried or those who have done a limited amount of cross country skiing. Some people feel that it is not necessary to have instruction in cross country since it does not seem particularly difficult and, after all, they are only interested in it for the fresh air and exercise. It is true that anyone can go out and walk on a pair of cross country skis, but if he takes a few lessons he can learn to slide his skis with more ease in a rhythmic step which will enable him to cover more distance and tire less easily from doing so. Further lessons will teach him climbing steps, different types of sliding steps for varying terrain, and downhill positions for safety when running straight downhill.

All of this will, of course, add a great deal to the enjoyment of the sport because the skier will be improving each time he goes out. After three or four lessons a beginner will have learned enough to go on a three- or four-mile cross country tour without getting too tired. He should not, however, go out alone unless he is on a marked track with check-in and check-out points.

EQUIPMENT

Skis

In general, cross country skiing is a great deal less expensive than alpine skiing, not only because there is no necessity for lifts and tows, but also because the equipment is much less costly. Basically speaking, there are three types of cross country skis: a competition model which is very narrow and light; a light touring ski which is a bit heavier than the racing ski and somewhat wider; and a regular touring ski which is still wider and a bit heavier than the light touring ski. A beginner will find it advantageous to assume the extra weight and use the regular touring ski because of its width and strength. The extra width gives more stability and better balance, and the strength will enable the skis to take more abuse as the beginner progresses. The light touring ski could be used by a person who has done a considerable amount of alpine skiing, because he has already developed a sense of balance and will enjoy its life and lightness. The competition ski is made for experienced runners who will be using it mainly in established tracks. Because of its extreme narrowness this ski is too difficult for any beginner or intermediate, particularly if it is to be used outside of a track.

As far as the length of the ski is concerned, you can't go too far wrong choosing a ski four inches below your wrist when reaching your arm into the air. Until recently most skis had wooden bottoms—usually birch or hickory. Birch is used on competition and light touring skis because it is lighter and holds wax better, whereas hickory is used for regular touring skis because it will stand more abuse. Now there are cross country skis on the market with bottoms similar to those on alpine skis—that is polyethylene of one type or another. The advantage of this is the especially good wearing and sliding qualities of such a base and the ease with which it may be waxed.

On any of these three models of skis it is important to look for a pair with edges made out of a plastic material. If the skis do not have edges the sides will wear and chip and make skiing more difficult. You should be able to pick up a good pair of regular touring skis for around $30 to $45, and a good light touring ski for around $50. Some of the top competition skis are priced anywhere from $70 to $100.

Bindings

Cross country bindings are very simple and although there are many brands they all work on the same principle. There are two basic types: one is a cable and is not as popular as it used to be; the other is a simple toe plate with a front clamp which fastens the front part of the sole securely to the ski and allows free lifting of the heel. When using this type of binding, it is important to have a small heel plate which prevents your heel from slipping off the ski. Some sets come with these plates but some do not. They should be purchased since they are absolutely necessary.

Boots

There are two types of boots for cross country—above the ankle and below the ankle—and either will do for the beginner. If you intend to do quite a bit of cross country skiing, it is worthwhile to invest in a good pair of shoes because they will last longer and give more support. They will also be more flexible and bend more easily. A good pair of boots may be purchased for around $30 to $40.

Poles

Poles are usually made out of bamboo and are very inexpensive
. . . usually around $7. Some aluminum poles are now appearing
which combine strength and lightness but these are a bit more
expensive. The pole should be long enough to reach under your
armpit when the tip is touching the floor, although some experienced runners may prefer a pole an inch or two longer. Ski shops
often sell a package of boots, skis, poles, and bindings for cross
country, which will save the beginner money and simplify things
for him.

Clothing

While it is not necessary to purchase special clothing for cross
country many people find their regular ski clothes too warm and
cumbersome and prefer the lightness and fit of cross country
clothes. For winter there are jackets and knickers which are wind-
proof but breathe well. Gloves made especially for cross country
are lighter and ventilated so that the hands will not perspire as
much as with regular ski gloves. A hat is a necessity and you may
wish to purchase one especially made for cross country—one
which is somewhat lighter in weight than your regular ski toque.
You will also need a small fanny pack for supplies such as a
scraper and wax, in case there is a change in the weather and you
must change your wax or your skis ice up and need scraping.

Wax

Don't make the mistake of trying to learn cross country skiing
without wax on your skis or without skis which are equipped with
a new material on the base to keep the skis from slipping backwards. Waxing has become much easier since new spray-type
waxes have been developed. They are very effective and certainly
good enough for all types of touring. Rub-on waxes which come
in small cans are also very effective, but these require some
experience and usually have to be melted with a blow torch after
they have been rubbed on. This process is particularly delicate if
snow conditions require that you use more than one wax. Waxing
is usually taught by the cross country instructor along with
lessons on technique. Recently, however, skis have been made
with bottoms which eliminate all waxing and which have proven
to be quite satisfactory for the beginner or intermediate.

Let's Get Started

BASIC SLIDING

The first step in cross country skiing is to learn a combination of walking and sliding. This is taught in a straight line in a track and without the use of poles. The arms are carried low and relaxed and the whole sliding step is a relaxed movement. The more you can get the forward ski to slide, the better. After five or ten minutes you will find that your balance has improved, and this will increase the length of your stride.

Standing with feet together the weight is placed on the right foot.

The left foot is slid ahead with a slightly bent knee.

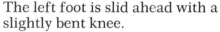

Now the weight is transferred and the right foot slides ahead, again with a slightly bent knee.

As the stride takes place, the heel of the back foot is lifted completely off the ski.

THE LONGER STRIDE

This sequence shows a longer stride. It can be practised continuously or done from a stop after each step.

With the body in a semi-crouch, the left foot is slightly ahead of the right foot and the entire weight is carried on the left foot.

As the right foot slides forward there is a strong push off with the left foot which increases the momentum and the distance of the slide.

While pushing off the back foot, the arms swing forward, the body rises, and the weight moves onto the forward ski.

DEVELOPING RHYTHM

This is an exercise in sliding to build up rhythm.

The poles are held in the centre and swung in rhythm alternately with each gliding step—much as in walking.

The arms should be extended each time to their full reach because this arm reach is an introduction to the use of the poles to propel the skier in later phases of cross country skiing.

As one foot slides forward, there is a lowering of the body to allow a strong push off with the back foot.

BASIC RUNNING DIAGONAL STRIDE (TWO-STEP)

The following is the basic two-step running sequence.

Now the stride is faster and there is more glide because of a strong push off with the back foot and the use of the poles to propel the body forward. Note the open and relaxed hand as the pole moves backward. This is important because it helps to relax the entire body.

THE SHORTENED DIAGONAL STRIDE

This is the same step as the previous one, but it has been shortened, so has the pole reach, in order to increase the gripping power and lessen the chance of back slipping. The degree of the shortening of the step and pole reach depends upon the snow conditions, the grade of the hill, and the holding quality of your wax.

The two-step is often used to climb a hill which is not too steep, although it can be used on a somewhat steeper hill if it is not too long. A short step is, of course, less tiring when used on a hill than a long step. Your movements should be extremely light and quiet.

TURNING WHILE CLIMBING DIAGONALLY

With proper wax a good runner in good condition can climb straight up a hill using a two or three step stride. However, to travel any length of hill using this method would be extremely tiring. A better method is to climb the hill diagonally, in which case it is necessary to learn to turn while ascending the hill.

In the following sequence I am showing a "step around turn." After considerable practice this turn can be done with almost no break in rhythm. A diagonal stride is shorter when climbing a hill than when crossing a flat. This allows the wax to grip better and enables the skier to get a stronger kick off with the back foot.

Start up the hill in a diagonal stride.

In preparation for the turn the feet are brought close together. The left pole is planted close to the left foot and the right pole comes forward.

In preparation for the turn the feet are brought close together. The left pole is planted close to the left foot and the right pole comes forward.
With both poles in the snow and the weight on the downhill ski, the left (or uphill) ski is brought around in a fluid movement close to the snow.

114

The weight has been transferred entirely to the downhill ski as the uphill ski is brought around and forward. The downhill knee is flexed and the body moves forward. With a strong thrust of the downhill pole and the downhill leg the opposite ski is slid forward and back into a diagonal stride. The turn should be fluid and continuous with almost no change in speed or rhythm.

DOUBLE-POLE GLIDE

This stride is used constantly while touring. It can be used to great advantage on a slight downgrade as it gives the skier extra speed and gives him a chance to rest because of the long glide. It may also be used on the flat for a change of pace and to relax the muscles. The correct timing of the push-off with the back foot and the double-pole push is very important. Another time that this stride may be used to advantage is when skiing on a flat and you come upon a slight descent in the terrain. A good runner will, of course, use this stride whenever he feels that it is advantageous, as in the previous instances or when encountering small bumps and hollows. With this stride it is possible for a good runner to glide 25-30 feet over flat terrain. The double pole glide is shown here on a very slight downgrade.

As the left foot comes forward in a two-step, both poles are extended to the front ready to be planted.

During the pole plant the right leg slides ahead. As it passes the left leg there is a strong push off with the left foot.

With a strong thrust of the poles the right leg moves forward and assumes the weight.

As the body passes the poles, the arms are extended in a follow through to the rear. This step can be repeated by bringing the left foot forward once again.

THE THREE-STEP STRIDE

A three-step may be used on the flat for a change of pace, but it is used to most advantage when diagonally climbing a long slope. The rhythm of this step is rather difficult to acquire and I would recommend lessons from a qualified instructor to anyone wishing to learn it. Once the step has been mastered the runner can go a long way without tiring. It is important to note in the following sequence how the downhill pole is planted twice in succession.

The left foot is moved forward and the downhill pole is planted for the first time.

With the aid of that pole, the right foot is now brought forward and the downhill pole is released, quickly brought forward, and planted again. As the second pole plant takes place, the uphill pole, which has been held aloft, is brought forward ready to plant.

As the left foot again comes forward the body is pulled up strongly with the aid of both poles which are planted in the snow.

The body passes the poles and the left foot is slid ahead into a glide, and the step is continued diagonally up the hill.

THE FOUR STEP STRIDE

The Four Step Stride is used sometimes for a change of pace on the flat but is used to most advantage when there is a slight downgrade in the terrain. The Four Step is four sliding steps, the first two without the use of the poles and the last two with the use of the poles.

This is an advanced movement in cross country and difficult to learn for the intermediate, mainly because of the timing of the pole action on the third and fourth steps. It is practically impossible to master without good instruction.

The best way to learn is to have an instructor demonstrate it side by side with the pupil on a parallel track. It is easier to demonstrate than explain.

In the following two pictures I have endeavoured to show how the poles move into position after the first two steps in preparation for their use in the third and fourth steps.

A fully accomplished cross country runner should be able to change from one type of stride to another without effort and use any one of them to the greatest advantage to suit the terrain.

CLIMBING STEEP SLOPES

Even with good wax there is a possibility while touring that you will encounter terrain too steep to ascend comfortably in a two-step. In this case here are two methods of climbing which may be used.

The herringbone is the easiest for a beginner or intermediate to learn. It is similar to that used in alpine skiing, except that a longer stride may be used because of the free lifting of the heels in cross country bindings. The herringbone is similar to walking but with the skis spread in a "V" and the poles used as an aid.

In the second method the movements are the same as in the herringbone except that the skis are kept apart and parallel. With each step the ski is stamped down solidly on its inside edge.

The only time this step should not be used is on very hard or icy surfaces. It is somewhat more difficult and takes more strength than the herringbone, but for an experienced runner it is the quicker method and in very soft snow almost as easy.

RIDING THE SKIS WHILE DESCENDING

Since cross country skis are more difficult to handle than alpine skis when descending a hill, a medium crouch position should always be maintained and the feet kept apart. This position will improve balance and the skis will be steadier and will track better.

BRAKING WHILE DESCENDING

At times you will come across terrain which is too difficult to *schuss* because of steepness or adverse snow conditions. In this event there is a safe method of descent which most people find rather fun. It is a very effective and safe method to use, particularly in a heavily wooded area. With feet apart both poles are placed between the legs with the baskets to the rear. The hands and poles are held close together and the body is lowered onto the poles in a sitting position. The more weight carried by the poles, the more braking power you will have. To resume speed simply assume a normal stance and remove the poles from between the legs.

122

DOWNHILL STEM CHRISTIE WITH OPEN STANCE

Whether doing a stem christie or a parallel turn on cross country skis, the skis should almost always be apart in a wide stance for stability, and the body should be centred as much as possible. A forward position on cross country skis is almost impossible because there is no downpull on the heels.

PARALLEL TURN IN UNBROKEN CORN SNOW

In this turn I have used *no* up-and-down motion. It is started with avalement.

Although flexion-extension can be used, the heels have a tendency to lift and pitch you forward, and so I feel avalement is preferable.

Notice how the body banks well into the hill due to the radius of the turn. This is made possible by the soft corn snow. Also notice the width of the stance.

CHANGING DIRECTION

There are many ways of changing direction from a standstill or while moving slowly, but the two methods shown are quick and enjoyable. Both should be practised from a standstill before attempted while moving. However, they should never be attempted while moving with any amount of speed. The jump turn is the easier of the two but the window turn is the more thrilling once mastered. It does, however, require considerably more strength in the arms.

Jump Turn

While moving slowly both poles are brought forward ready to plant and the knees are flexed.

Both poles are planted firmly in the snow, and the upper body faces slightly downhill.

The skis are jumped and turned around the inside pole while the outside pole is released.

When the new direction is reached the knees are extended to absorb shock upon landing.

Window Turn (*Gelände Turn*)

From a standing position and with both poles planted in the snow the heels are raised.

With strong support of the poles, both feet are kicked forward and up. As the tails of the skis pass the poles the skis are turned into the new direction.

Upon landing the outside pole has been released from the snow and the knees are in a position to absorb shock.

LUNGING

Lunging is used when going from one type of snow condition to another, or when encountering sudden drop-offs such as small cornices and mounds of snow. In this sequence I am dropping over a very steep mound of snow with a sharp hollow at the bottom.

Both arms are held to the side for balance and one foot is slid well ahead carrying most of the weight. With the heel completely off the ski, the rear knee is fully bent and almost touching the ski.

The same position is held while dropping over the crest, with most of the weight still on the forward ski.

Approaching the hollow the body rises considerably.

As the transition in the snow is encountered, the body lowers and much of the weight is transferred to the back foot to keep the tips of the skis from sinking and pitching the skier forward in the soft snow.

TELEMARK

A telemark turn has been well known to cross country skiers for many years. If it is demonstrated by an expert it can be an extremely graceful turn to watch, especially when executed in deep snow. It can be used wherever a stem christie or a parallel turn is used, although it is a bit more difficult to execute if the surface is very hard. The telemark turn is shown here on rather soft spring snow.

The body assumes a lunge position with most of the weight on the forward ski.

The arms are carried to the side for balance and the forward ski is turned onto its inside edge. The turn begins with a strong steering action of the forward knee and leg.

As the turn continues, notice the position of the tip of the inside ski in relation to the outside foot and how the outside arm is projecting forward in a circular motion.

At the end of the turn the inside ski is slid parallel to the outside ski. Throughout the entire turn the heel of the front foot is flat on the ski and the rear heel is lifted as high as possible.